Catholic School Kids Say the Funniest Things

Mary Kathleen Glavich, S.N.D.
illustrated by Christopher Fay

Paulist Press
New York/Mahwah, N.J.

Cover art and interior illustrations by Christopher Fay

Cover design by Valerie Petro

Library of Congress Cataloging-in-Publication Data

Glavich, Mary Kathleen.
    Catholic school kids say the funniest things / Mary Kathleen Glavich.
        p. cm.
    ISBN 0-8091-4106-X
    1. Schools—Humor. 2. Education—Humor. 3. Catholics—Humor. I. Title.
    PN6231.S3 G59 2002
    818'.02—dc21

                                                            2002006215

Published by Paulist Press
997 Macarthur Boulevard
Mahwah, New Jersey 07430

www.paulistpress.com

Printed and bound in the United States of America

Contents

To all those consecrated women who handed on the faith through the Catholic school system with courage, perseverance, and a twinkle in their eye!

Introduction

In the year 2000 my community of the Sisters of Notre Dame celebrated its sesquicentennial. We are a teaching order. For 150 years we have passed on our faith and its traditions through education, especially in Catholic schools. We have also taught English, math, and other survival skills to children and adults. Sometimes we have been successful and sometimes not.

Teaching is a challenge and an awful lot of hard work. It is serious business. As with any career, though, teaching has its lighter moments. Often, over dinner, the sisters in the community entertain one another with funny things the students (or we ourselves) have said and done in the classroom. Sometimes while correcting papers, we run to a coworker to share a particularly ridiculous answer to a question. Parents have told us school-related stories that made us laugh to the point of tears. From time to time we remark, "We should write these down."

This book is a collection of humorous stories gleaned from the memories of the Sisters of Notre Dame. Some of them are classics that have been handed down in our community for years. Others are as recent as this year. Only a few names have been changed.

♥

Anyone associated with schools—teachers, students, and parents—will be able to identify with the stories here. Who has not clapped erasers, stood in the corner, been laughed at for mispronouncing a word, or gotten nervous at a supervisor's visit?

Those who are familiar with Catholic schools and Sisters will find these anecdotes especially enjoyable. The stories evoke memories of drinking chocolate milk after a school Mass, selling candy bars, hearing the click of Sister's rosary, offering up spiritual bouquets, and celebrating the pastor's name day.

As every child learns in religion class, joy is one of the fruits of the Holy Spirit. Joy is a hallmark of holiness. May this little book bring you much joy and laughter. It is our gift to you in honor of our jubilee.

Mary Kathleen Glavich, S.N.D.

First Days

School Daze

It was the first day of school. Sister Caron's first graders were used to the kindergarten schedule of only a half day of school. When lunchtime came, one child was ready to go home. Sister said, "No, you can't go home. You have to stay the whole day."

Disgusted, the child grumbled, "Who the hell signed me up for this?"

Off to an Unpromising Start

At the end of the first day of school, Sister Karlene ushered a group of her kindergartners to the bus. When she returned to the classroom, a little boy asked, "Are you the one who was in our class all day?"

Sister thought: If he doesn't know **me**, how will he manage the alphabet?

Eager Beaver

On the first day of school, Sister Harold explained the daily routine. She said, "When I tap the bell, we'll all stand and say a little prayer."

An eager voice rang out, "Sister, don't make it two decades, just one. I want to get going."

Innocent

The preschool children were playing "Who Stole the Cookie from the Cookie Jar?" in order to learn one another's names. Finally someone chose Brian for his turn by chanting the line, "Did Brian steal the cookie from the cookie jar?" Brian began to cry and said, "I'd never do that!" It took a while to convince him that it was only a game.

Tabled

In one school the cafeteria tables folded into the walls to convert the room into a large social hall. A watchful teacher supervising the lunch period noticed that every day one group of first graders rushed through their lunch. On investigating, she discovered that they were afraid of being folded into the walls with the tables!

A Quick Cure

One morning, a few days after school had started, a first grader had an attack of school-phobia. He cried and cried for his mommy and refused to go into the classroom. In desperation, Sister Lisa, the principal, summoned another first-grade boy who had also suffered such an attack on the first day of school. She asked him, "Remember how you had such a hard time leaving your mother? What could John do?"

Both boys sat down on the steps. The boy who had recovered counseled John, "We have to do work, and your mommy has to do work. So let's get to work." With that the two boys got up and walked into the classroom.

Mass

Good Discipline

Sister Mary Adelle was perturbed. Father was giving the homily at the school Mass, and one of her second graders in the front row was talking and fooling around. Not wanting to cause a disturbance by walking to the front, Sister just leaned forward and in a loud whisper said, "Neil!" Immediately her whole class knelt.

Intercession for Life

The second graders were gathered for a school Mass. A child who was new to the school walked in late and sat at the end of the first pew. He had been to the practice for the liturgy, so he had a little idea of what was going on. When it came time for the intercessions, he marched up to the lectern and prayed, "For the birds and the bees, let us pray to the Lord."

Hearing Things

The school was gathered in church waiting for Mass to begin. One of the fourth graders walked back to her teacher and held out a ring. She said, "Sister, someone left this in the first pewk."

7

The Mute Button

During a rather long homily at a school Mass, a boy in the front row of Sister Adelle's class began talking. Not wanting to cause a commotion, Sister directed the child seated next to her to go up and tell him to stop talking. He dutifully walked down the aisle, past the pews, and stopped in front of the lectern. Looking up at the priest, he declared, "Sister said you should stop talking."

Fidelity

One day dignitaries from the Notre Dame community joined the school for its weekly Mass. The second-grade teacher was concerned because the student who was to read the responsorial psalm had not arrived. To remedy the situation, Sister asked her best reader to be a substitute.

At the appointed time, when the reader who had practiced still had not shown up, the substitute walked up to the lectern and proclaimed the responsorial verse: "The fiddle-dee-dee of the Lord remains forever." The whole school, including the eighth graders, calmly repeated this refrain and continued to repeat it to the end of the psalm.

Making Peace

The first graders were at the school Mass for the first time. After the sign of peace, Sister noticed that five-year-old Michael was rubbing his eyes, and she wondered whether he was crying. She went to his pew, and sure enough, there were tears running down his face. "What's wrong, Michael?" she asked.

"Nobody shook my hand," he said. Sister shook his hand.

Liturgy Pageant

A deacon was giving the homily at a school Mass. He pointed to the stole crossed over his left shoulder and questioned, "Does anyone know what this means?"

Immediately, a first-grade girl raised her hand. Sister whispered, "Put your hand down. You don't know."

"Yes, I do," the girl declared.

"No, you don't," Sister argued.

"Yes, I do," the girl insisted.

The deacon said, "Little girl who's making such a fuss, what does this mean?"

Loud and clear the girl proclaimed, "Miss America!"

Religion

Who's Confused?

The third graders were reviewing the gifts God gave our first parents. There was one more gift to mention—namely, infused knowledge. Martin's face lit up and he waved his hand excitedly. When Sister called on him, he stated, "God gave Adam and Eve confused knowledge."

Guest Appearance

A family with a small boy visited the school chapel. The mother pointed to the tabernacle and whispered to her son, "Jesus is in there."

Curious, the boy asked, "When's he coming out?"

Old Testament Fairy Tales

Sister Barbara's sixth-grade CCD class was reviewing some Old Testament stories. One lad, recounting the story of Joshua and the battle of Jericho, got his tales mixed up. "The Israelites surrounded the town of Jericho," he said. "Then they huffed and they puffed, and they blew the walls down."

A Good Guess

Sister Elizabeth gave her children a test on the coming of Jesus. One child was weak in theology but strong in logic. In answer to the question, **When the angel asked Mary to be the Mother of God, what did she say?** he wrote, **Why me?**

Lucifer's Replacement

The pastor asked the young students, "Who was the leader of the bad angels?" Sheila was sure she knew. She waved her hand furiously. When Father called on her, she blurted out, "The bogeyman!"

Forbidden Dentures

The pastor was seeing whether the first graders remembered the previous lesson he had taught. Unfortunately, he called on Christina, who had been absent for the lesson. He asked her to recite the first commandment. In response to her blank look, Father gave the child a helpful start. He prompted, "I am the Lord your God."

No response.

Again he tried, "I am the Lord your God. You shall not..."

Still no response.

Yet again, "I am the Lord your God. You shall not have false..."

This time Christina's face lit up. "Teeth?" she asked hopefully.

P is for Perplexing

Sister Barbara was discussing the last days of Jesus with the first graders. "Jesus went to Jerusalem for a special feast day. What was it? It begins with **p**."

"St. Patrick's Day!" one youngster volunteered.

"No," replied Sister.

Another child raised his hand. "Thanksgiving," he said.

In a scornful voice, a classmate commented, "What a dumb answer. The pilgrims never went to Jerusalem!"

Mixed Vegetables

Father was reviewing the story of Our Lord's passion with the children. He asked, "What was the name of the garden Jesus and his apostles went to after the Last Supper?" A boy's hand shot up. He was not one who usually knew the answers.

"Do you really know?" asked Father, surprised.

"Yes," said the boy confidently. "The Garden of Pickles."

"Close," granted the priest.

Revenge

The second graders were talking about the virtues of Jesus and how we should imitate him.

Sister said, "When people hurt you, act like Jesus. Give them another chance. Forgive them." Then she asked, "But what if the person who hurts you is really mean and doesn't like you at all? Think: What would Jesus do then?"

The answer came quickly: "He'd send them straight to hell."

Catholics in the Temple

One of Sister Anelle's CCD students read the Bible with a modern mind. He wondered why Jesus chased people out of the Temple for playing Bingo.

Then There's the Pumpkin Eater

Sister Colette was going to tell her first graders a gospel story about Jesus and the apostle Peter. To introduce the story she asked, "Does anyone know who Peter was?" One boy timidly raised his hand and answered with a lisp, "I think he wath a wabbit."

Like the Cheshire Cat

One child knew the comic strips better than he knew the Bible. When Sister asked, "Who was the angel that appeared to Mary at the time of the Annunciation?" this student answered, "Garfield."

Morale Support for a Bishop

To welcome the new bishop, Sister Josephmarie invited the students in her school to write him letters. At the end of the day, among the letters piled on her desk, she found an intimate one from a fourth grader that read, "Now I know you are a new bishop and so you are probably very nervous. But don't be. I'll tell you a secret. I'm praying for you."

Another fourth grader failed to grasp his teacher's explanation of a diocese. In his letter, after telling the bishop all his favorite jokes, he closed with, "Your fellow-diocese, Tim."

Sneaking up on Jesus

A teacher traveling to church with her small students reminded them to walk quietly, especially going up the creaky stairs. She said, "Try to be so quiet that even Jesus will be surprised we're coming." The children obeyed conscientiously. They tiptoed to the church and opened the door. Suddenly, one child gleefully shouted, "Surprise!"

Turning up the Heat

During the severe winter months of 1977, a gas shortage made it difficult to heat the schools, and the children of St. Mary's had to share a building with a neighboring public school, Avon East. One public school teacher prepared her students to accept the children from St. Mary's. After she finished, one boy raised his hand. He wanted to inform his classmates about what to expect.

"You know what?" he said seriously. "The children from the Catholic school are really different from us. If I would hit one of them on the cheek, he would turn the other cheek."

Hearing about this, the Sisters at St. Mary's prayed, "Dear God, please don't let any of our children be put to the test."

The Living Dead

Assuming her students learned about vocations in previous years, Sister Bernadel asked them to name the states in life. One seventh grader supplied the answer, "There are three states in life: religious, married, and dead."

Trapped

During a unit on religious life, some eighth graders were amazed to learn about the cloister, a monastery where outsiders do not enter and the religious usually do not leave.

"Gee, Sister," Dan asked, "don't they get cloisterphobia?"

Reading
and Phonics

A Couple of Meanings

The primary-grade teacher was discussing a story about hats. When she came to the line that referred to hats for brides and hats for grooms, she asked, "What's a groom?" One child answered brightly, "That's when your dog gets a haircut."

A Good Try

During a phonics game Mary said, "I'm thinking of a word that begins with the letter **G**."

"Are you thinking of the word **Jesus**?" asked Frank.

"Jesus begins with a **J**," Mary replied.

Then Bette guessed, "Are you thinking of the word **God**?"

Frank immediately challenged, "Isn't Jesus God?

"Yes," answered Mary, "but God spells his name with a **G**."

A Close Call

First-year teacher Sister Mary Bruce was concerned about a story in her reader. One of the characters was a dog named Wee Brucie. Not looking forward to being called Wee Brucie by her children for the rest of the year, Sister asked the principal for a different set of readers. No, it was too expensive to buy another set.

The day finally arrived when the dreaded story was to be read. The boy who was reading aloud came to the sentence that introduced the dog Wee Brucie. He pronounced the name Wee Brucky. No one batted an eye or corrected him—including Sister.

All-Purpose Room

Sister Barbara was preparing her fourth graders to read a story in which the parlor of a house was mentioned. Realizing that many of the modern children would not be familiar with the word **parlor**, Sister Barbara asked what a parlor is. Vince replied, "Where you're either laid out or get your hair cut."

A Haven in Distress

Sister Pamela, a principal, received a note from a teacher that read, "Nathan left for the washroom and has not come back." Upon arriving at the boys' washroom, Sister found that the outer doors, which were usually open, were closed and the lights were off. She called, "Nathan, are you here?"

"Yes, Sister," came the answer.

"Do you feel all right?"

"Yes, Sister," Nathan
replied.

"Your teacher is worried about you," Sister said. "When are you going back to the classroom?"

"Is phonics almost over?"

Language Arts

Gardening Secrets

The school was undergoing an evaluation. As part of the process, the students were asked to write answers to questions on an evaluation sheet. In response to the question, "What do you think of your school plant?" one child wrote, "There are many plants in our school. I don't know which one is the school plant."

Misnomer

As the first graders were walking through the junior high hall, one young fellow remarked, "I don't know why they call this a high hall. It's no higher than our hall."

School, Zoo, or Morgue?

The principal, in her announcements to the school, stated that the forms that the teachers had distributed were to be taken home and filled out. She concluded by saying, "The deadline is Friday."

A little boy dutifully brought the form home to his mother, then broke the exciting news, "Friday there's going to be a dead lion in school! Mom, what's a dead lion doing in school?"

Daffynition

Sister Barbara gives Mike credit for creative thinking. When she asked, "What is an aqueduct?" he answered, "It's something like a seal, but it has webbed feet."

A Major Difference

On the playground, a primary-level boy was praised by a teacher for observing a certain school policy. He ran to his own teacher and excitedly told her that another Sister wanted to condemn him.

(**Commend** maybe?)

Underestimating

Sister Regina was carrying on a conversation about dinosaurs with some primary-grade children. She figured that in talking with such little ones, she should speak on a level only slightly higher than baby talk. When a lad showed her a model of a particular dinosaur, she asked, "Oooh, do you think he'd eat me?"

"Oh, no," replied the little boy. "He's not carnivorous."

Wee Spell

The eighth-grade cheerleaders were the idols of the first graders. During recess, Sister St. Gerard heard the little ones imitating them. The leader asked, "Give me a **B**," and the aspiring cheerleaders shouted "**B!**" The game went on.

"Give me a **Q!**"

"**Q.**"

"Give me an **R!**"

"**R.**"

Finally the leader asked, "What does it spell?" and one tot called out, "I don't know!"

A Budding Novelist

After developing the week's spelling words, an upper-grade teacher told the students to write a short paragraph using five or more of the words. Ten minutes later the following paragraph was handed in:

"In the **aisles** of the **vehicle**, we found piles of **rhubarb**. The **colonel** asked the **shepherds** to help him clean it up, but the shepherds had **asthma**."

Sister had neglected to add that the paragraph should make sense.

College Demons

When Sister Immaculee taught the seventh graders that **all right** was two words, and that one of them was spelled with two l's, she remarked, "This is one of those spelling demons. What's a demon?" Mike raised his hand and said, "I know what a demon is. It's the head of a college. My sister teaches in the college in Toledo, and they have one down there."

Mathematics

New Math

Sister Karlene was assigned to teach kindergarten. When one of her kindergartners was reciting his facts at home, his mother was shocked to hear him saying, "One plus one, the son of a bitch is two. Two plus two, the son of a bitch is four." Mom called Dad over to verify what she was hearing. A phone call to Sister Karlene clarified that she had taught the children, "One plus one, the sum of which is two," and so on.

Superstork

A second grader was elated by the arrival of a new baby sister, the first girl in a family of boys. Sister asked, "How much does she weigh, Tommy?" The reply came, "Eight quarts."

Light Dawns

Sister St. Martha taught algebra to gifted students. One Monday morning, however, the students were not paying attention. In frustration, Sister looked around the room and complained, "I might as well be talking to the lights." One punster in the back of the room quipped, "At least they're bright."

Snow Job

A first grader was caught throwing snowballs. The principal, Sister Jane Therese, issued the punishment. During the noon break the little boy was to make fifty snowballs and put them in a straight line. After some time, the culprit called Sister to see his handiwork. Alas, he had arranged the snowballs in a serpentine design.

Sister said, "No, this won't do. Put them in five rows with ten in each row."

After school, Sister overheard the child telling a friend, "Don't ever throw snowballs around this place. If you do, she makes you put them into sets and subsets."

One Plus One

Plural forms can be tricky. Sister Meribeth was drilling her second graders on the rules. At one point she threw in a hard word to stump them. She asked, "What is the plural of solo?" Expecting a child to answer s-o-l-o-s or s-o-l-o-e-s, Sister was dumbfounded when a boy called out, "Duet!"

Basic Facts

After years of teaching calculus, Sister Patricia was assigned to teach a general math class. On the first day, she instructed the class to take out a sheet of paper. As the students placed sheets of notebook paper on their desks, Sister heard a girl near the front mutter, "I can never remember which side the holes go on."

"It's going to be a long year," Sister sighed to herself.

Science and
Health

Spotted Skin

Sister Grace is Irish and has a generous sprinkling
of freckles. One day she learned a little more
about cultural diversity when a
Hispanic student asked
with concern, "Do those
spots hurt?"

Twins?

During lunch in the school cafeteria a small girl revealed to her classmates that her birthday was July fourth, so her family called her a firecracker. The principal overheard this. She whispered in the girl's ear, "I was born on July fourth, too."

The child looked up at Sister wide-eyed and asked, "How did you get to be so big so fast?"

A for Effort

During class the fourth graders had time to read books of their choice independently. Sister Helen Louise noticed one girl was engrossed in the book **The Scarlet Letter**. She walked over to the child, intending to explain that her book was more suitable for high-school-aged students. The girl looked up guiltily and proved the point by admitting in a whisper, "I know it's a bad book. It's about a girl who had a baby before she was pregnant."

Whew!

During a science lesson Sister Mary St. Jude told her eighth graders that if they had questions about the reproductive system they should ask their parents. That day after school one girl who had a brother in the second grade said, "Sister, you should have been at our house last night. My brother asked my dad what sex was. Dad sent him to Mom. She sent him back to Dad because Jimmy asked him first."

The girl explained that in the end her dad asked his son, "Why do you want to know?" Jimmy replied, "Because in my wallet there's a card to fill out, and one of the lines says 'Sex.'"

Protector of the Innocent

One day Bobby came to his teacher and said, "Sister, I hurt my back when I was thrown from the merry-go-round."

"How did that happen?" Sister inquired.

"No one was to blame," said Bobby. "It was the centrifugal force that threw me off."

A Sad Story

Sister Mary Ann was reading a story to a group of preschoolers. It was a very hot day. Suddenly one youngster observed, "Sister, there are tears on your forehead."

A Word of Caution

Sister Donnalee took her second graders outdoors for a hike. Coming across milkweed, the children asked what it was. Sister told them and squeezed some milk out.

A little while later, some children told her, "Timmy's crying."

"Why?" Sister asked.

"Because he licked the milk. We told him it's poison, so he's going to get sick."

By the time the students returned to the classroom, Timmy had stopped crying but was still and silent and indeed looked sick. Sister Donnalee sent him to the principal, who sent him to the school nurse, escorted by Michael, a third grader. The next day, Timmy was fine. That morning Michael, who had been a notorious student in Sister's class the previous year, came to her and said in a serious voice, "I'd like to give you a tip. Don't take your children to dangerous places."

Buried Treasure

An inner-city school was given seeds by the city's garden club so that the children could plant flowers and vegetables at home. As the culmination of the project, the school had a garden day. The children could bring in either pictures of their garden or actual produce. One child, on seeing the carrots that another child had produced, exclaimed, "Oh, we brought in leaves like that, but we didn't know they had carrots at the bottom!"

History and Geography

A Clever Bluff

In history class Sister Barbara asked her eighth-grade students for the definition of "privateer." Not knowing the answer, Dan responded, "How about an undercover Mickey Mouse fan?"

A Capital Answer

The fifth grade was practicing the states and their capitals by playing Traveler. A child stood beside another child's desk. Both were eager to name the state that matched the capital Sister Regina called out. The first one to give the right answer moved to stand by the next child's desk. At one point during the game Sister said, "Concord."

Instantly, one contestant called out, "Grapes!"

A Living Fossil

A four-year-old asked her teacher, "Are you older than my father?"

"Yes," Sister Myra said.

"Are you older than my grandfather?" the child continued.

"Yes," said Sister, who knew the grandfather.

"Then," concluded the girl, "you must be older than the dinosaurs."

Art and
Music

Piano Exercise

Nhi was a second grader who spoke Vietnamese at home. One day she came for her piano lesson before Sister Ellen was ready. Sister directed, "Nhi, go to the piano and warm up." A few moments later Sister looked up and saw Nhi behind the piano doing jumping-jacks! The little girl had learned about warm-ups in phys ed class.

Change of Voice

Jimmy was in the choir and sang a special song for the Christmas Midnight Mass. On the first day back at school, he asked his teacher, "Sister, did you hear a squeak during the song? Because I think I squoke."

Improvised Band Music

Sister Marisa's second graders were having a science lesson. Holding one end of a rubber band in their teeth, the children were to stretch it and then pluck it in order to hear various tones. As the children did this, the room was filled with the sound of rubber-band music. Suddenly there was an odd "Plink." One lad's loose front tooth had shot out onto the floor.

Giving Away
the Whole Word

The first graders were having a music lesson. Tom was asked to identify the kind of note Sister was pointing to. "Tell me the first letter of the name, Sister," he pleaded.

"**W**," answered the teacher. That didn't help. Tom begged to be told another letter.

"**H**," the Sister said grudgingly. This hint shed no light either. After much persuasion, Sister finally revealed the next letter, namely **O**.

"Long **O** or short?" Tom asked.

A Surrogate Mother

The kindergarten teacher saw to it that her children's clothes were protected during art lessons. She explained to them that they wore aprons so their mothers wouldn't have to wash paint out of their clothes.

One day, during a messy art lesson, the teacher got paint on her clothes. A little girl commented, "You're your own mudder, aren't you?"

A Trick on the Teacher

For an art project Sister Kathleen planned to have her first graders make papier-mâché heads of what they were going to be for Halloween. She had read that adding grease to white glue makes a good mixture for papier-mâché. On the day of the art lesson, a teacher's aide appeared wearing a beautiful suit and high heels. She helped the children dip the strips of newspaper into the super-gooey mixture and drape them over the balloons.

All was going well until a child's balloon suddenly burst and went flying around the room, hitting the new flashcard chart and leaving a grease mark. Soon other balloons laden with strips of newspaper began careening around the room. The balloons were too thin to hold the sopping paper. At the end of the day only a piece of red balloon dangling from the ceiling remained as a reminder of the tragedy. The teacher's aide never returned.

A Thimple Thuggethion

Sister Marian's second graders were cutting and pasting during an art lesson at the end of the school day. When the bell rang to prepare for dismissal, several children weren't finished with their projects yet.

Colleen came to Sister and said, "Thithter, if you would thtop before the bell ringth, we wouldn't get tho exthited when the bell ringth!" From that day on, Sister never scheduled art as the last lesson of the day.

Teachers

Tongue-Twisters

One year the students in Sister Kathleen's English classes had particularly unusual names. It required real effort to keep Lavitha, Latonya, and LaRonda straight. Also in the class were a girl named Basilica and a girl named Parthenia. One day when Parthenia raised her hand, Sister's wires crossed and she called, "Parthenon?"

A Slow Student

During indoor recess the third and fourth graders were playing school. Taking part in the game, the teacher, Sister Janet, sat at a child's desk. Adam, who was playing the teacher, came up to her and asked, "And just how many years have you been kept back?"

Double Meaning

Sister Luke, a sweet, elderly nun, was telling her students that on the previous day part of a ceiling had fallen. "I was standing in the classroom, and suddenly I got plastered," she innocently said.

A Greenhorn

For her first year of teaching, Sister Agnesmarie, a city girl, was assigned to fifth graders in a rural school. During one lesson she explained to her students that food is stored in a silo so that the animals will have food in the winter.

"What do they store in the silo?" asked Sister. Hands flew up. "All right, Terence, what do they put in the silo?"

"They put fodder up there," Terence answered.

Fodder was not in Sister's vocabulary at that time. "Terence," she said firmly, "are you trying to be funny? We are not talking about your father."

A Cover-Up

As she began showing the filmstrip for her senior class, Sister Barbara Ann realized that she had threaded it the wrong way. The reversed words on each frame were unreadable. Thinking quickly, Sister explained to the students, "Words sometimes distract us from the visual impact of a filmstrip. We will view this filmstrip with the words blurred so that we can better absorb the message as a whole." With dignity intact, Sister proceeded to show the filmstrip.

The Teacher Who Failed

Sister Maretta, the principal, was hard up for a substitute for the first grade. A former eighth-grade teacher, she gritted her teeth and went in to spend the day with the first graders herself. As the morning dragged on, it became obvious that she was having a difficult time keeping the class occupied with worksheets. One little boy sighed and helpfully suggested, "Why don't we all just go home?" And Sister thought, "My sentiments exactly."

A Know-Nothing Nun

The high school students were in study hall. One of them approached Sister LeRoy with a question. Sister couldn't answer. The girl returned to her seat. A while later, the girl came to Sister again with another question. Again Sister couldn't answer. Exasperated, the girl exclaimed, "Gee, don't you know geometry either?"

In the Eye of the Beholder

The kindergartners were allowed to celebrate their birthdays by wearing special clothes to school. On their teacher's birthday, she decided to dress up too. Her efforts were rewarded when one little boy declared in awe, "Oh, Miss Hall, you are so pretty." With emphasis, he repeated, "You are so-o-o pretty." Then to convince her of his utter admiration, he said, "You are as pretty as Miss Piggy."

Equals

Sister Teresemarie often engaged a high school student named Tom in conversation about theology. He was eager to learn. One day after school, when the boy had finished

cleaning the chemistry lab and Sister had finished doing her convent housework, the two met at the incinerator with their respective garbage. Tom immediately greeted her with, "Well, Sister, we meet again, but now on the same level."

Great Expectations

The phone rang and Sister Regina answered.

"I'd like to speak to a teacher," a voice said.

"This is a teacher," Sister replied.

"Well, could you tell me the name of the third-largest Hawaiian island?"

"No," said Sister.

"Are you a teacher?" the voice asked again.

"Yes," Sister assured the caller.

"Well, what is the name of the third-largest Hawaiian island?" the voice repeated.

"I don't know," Sister admitted.

"Oh," the person replied, and then inquired, "Is there a **real** teacher there I could speak to?".

Especially about Sisters

St. Sister

A curious fifth grader asked her teacher, "Sister, what was your name before you were canonized?"

Besting God

One of Sister Myra's preschoolers announced, "When I grow up, I'm going to marry you."

Showing the child the plain silver band on her ring finger, Sister said, "Your mother has a wedding ring like this. What does it mean?"

"That she belongs to my dad," the little boy answered.

"My ring means that I belong to God," Sister explained.

Undaunted, the boy replied, "Well, I'd get you one with a stone."

On a Pedestal

When the Sisters opened their first school in Memphis, the children were very curious about them. One day a group of ragamuffins rang the convent doorbell to meet some of the unfamiliar creatures in the long, black robes. As they conversed with the Sister who answered the door, one child declared, "We saw your statue in church this morning."

The Name Game

In the past, a Sister's real name, as opposed to her religious name, was always a challenging mystery. One seventh-grade teacher was approached by a student whose cousin knew Sister's uncle's brother-in-law who worked with the cousin's great-aunt.

"Your last name's Maver, isn't it?" the student asked.

"Yes," Sister conceded.

"Aha!" the triumphant boy responded. "Now I only have to figure out your first name."

A Winner

Notre Dame Elementary
School is located in the
Sisters' provincial house. The
same large building houses the faculty, Sisters in
formation, and the sick Sisters. Behind the building
is the Sisters' cemetery.

To celebrate National Catholic Schools Week, an
essay contest was held. Students were to write on
the topic, "What makes my school special." An entry
from a fifth grader at Notre Dame began: "In our
school we bury the dead teachers in the field behind
the gym." Needless to say, this entry did not make it
to the finals.

A Heavenly Teacher

Sister Mary Jo tried to get her second graders to imagine what heaven was like. There wasn't much of a response. Finally a little boy in the back raised his hand and suggested, "Aw, Sister. You've been there. Why don't you just tell us about it?"

Rechristened

Sister Mary St. Hugh's unfamiliar name has been garbled by many a first grader. Once a little girl went home on the first day of school and announced to her family that her teacher was Sister Mary Who. However, Sister prefers her frequent misnomer, Sister Mary Hug.

A Postulant Defined

In former days many girls entered the convent directly after high school. These girls, called postulants, usually attended college. Nancy, having entered the convent at an older age and being a certified teacher already, was assigned to teach. She wore the postulant's garb: a black cape and a black skirt.

Shortly after school began, one of Nancy's fifth graders was overheard explaining to a friend, "My teacher is half a sister and half a lady, but every inch a teacher."

A VIP

The community's superior general, who lived in Rome, was coming to visit the school. All the children had been prepared for her visit. Kevin, a kindergartner, conveyed the news to his parents by translating it into kindergartner**speak**. He announced, "Tomorrow the queen of the Sisters is coming to visit."

Anything for an Arby's

On the way home Sister Sebastien stopped at Arby's for a sandwich and a shake. As she waited, the man behind the counter said, "Your food's been paid for."

"By whom?" Sister asked.

The young man nodded at a gentleman in a car at the drive-through window who was grinning at Sister. She waved her thanks.

The next day, Sister was telling her first graders about God's goodness. She gave the example of the man's goodness to her. One child asked, "Did you have your hat on?"

"Yes," Sister replied, "I always wear my veil."

Then very seriously, Michael stated, "Tonight I'm going to pray to God to change me into a girl so that I can become a nun like you."

Students

Consumer Children

The kindergarten teacher gave her class a worksheet on the letter **b**. She directed them to put a check in front of each word that began with **b**. "Do you understand the directions?" she asked. "Yes," they said. However, as the teacher walked around the class she found that instead of a checkmark, some children were marking the **b** words by drawing a horizontal box with scribbles and lines inside. What was it? A bank check, of course.

A Kind Assist

Sister had told her first graders a story about a coming feast day. Later, intending to review the lesson, she asked if anyone wanted to help her tell the story. Alphonse, the tallest boy in the room, raised his hand and came shuffling up to the front from the last row. He stood in front of the teacher's desk, turned to Sister, and said, "I'd like to help you, Sister. Where are you stuck?"

Self-Defense

At the Montessori school a three-year-old was having difficulty buttoning his coat. Sister Doloretta said to an older child, "Would you please help that little boy?"

Offended, the little boy stretched to his maximum height, thrust both hands in his pockets, and said, "I am a **big** boy."

Quickly Sister amended her request to, "Will the bigger boy please help the big boy with his coat?" She was rewarded with a smile on the face of the big boy.

Surprise Parties

While checking the children's records, Sister asked Kim when his birthday was. He was perplexed for a while but soon recovered his composure and replied, "Oh, Sister, I really don't know. It always comes as a surprise to me."

A Simple Solution

A little boy with the last name of Butts was constantly being teased by his classmates. One day he came home from school and begged his mother, "Mom, can I change my last name to something simpler—like Rodriguez?"

Proposed Promotion

Alex was an unusually bright second grader. One day after Alex gave a correct answer, a classmate commented, "Alex should be an adult. He knows so much."

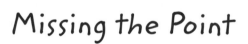

Missing the Point

The second grader came up to Sister Sharon's desk and said, "I have to go to the bathroom."

Sister corrected him in a whisper, "May I please go to the bathroom."

"Do you have to go too?" he asked.

Checkmate

Sister Margaret had once been a high school principal and a school supervisor. Now as she neared retirement, she enjoyed working with young children at a parish grade school. The kindergartners knew that if they wanted to join the school chess club they first had to beat Sister at checkers. One day a 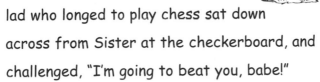 lad who longed to play chess sat down across from Sister at the checkerboard, and challenged, "I'm going to beat you, babe!"

And he did.

The Birds and the Bees

Little Viola's eyes sparkled as
she skipped into
the classroom one morning,
eager to tell Sister the
wonderful news.

"Sister," she crowed,
"Mommy laid a baby last
night!"

A Pony Tale

The superintendent of schools was visiting the school. He stopped in the first-grade classroom where the children were reading a story about a pony. Sister Roseann asked the children if they thought Monsignor had ever ridden on a pony. The children answered, "No, Sister."

But Monsignor interrupted and said, "I did, when I was a little boy."

One fellow, sizing up the priest's robust form, remarked, "But you couldn't ride one now, because you'd squash the poor pony."

Monsignor laughed heartily, to Sister's relief.

Moral Support

The new diocesan social studies curriculum was implemented in Sister Rita Mary's classroom. On the day diocesan officials were coming to observe the children, one little girl asked Sister, "What do we do if we get nervous?"

Sister replied, "Look at me and I'll smile at you. Then you won't be nervous."

Promptly another girl reassured Sister, "And when you get nervous, Sister, just look at me, and I'll smile at you."

Parents

Removing Old Leaves

For open house the third graders had placed booklets of their work on their desks for their parents to see. Jimmy had prudently removed those papers of his which weren't very good. His mother, however, noticed that his booklet was much smaller than the other children's. When she asked him about it, Jimmy explained the missing papers: "I did those before my improvement."

Relief

The junior-high students and their parents attended an evening session on sex education presented by a doctor and a nurse. At the conclusion the presenters encouraged the students to ask their parents any questions they might have. Afterwards one father and son were driving home alone when the son said, "Dad, I was wondering..."

Dad's heart began racing, and his knuckles turned white on the steering wheel. What was his son going to ask? How would he answer?

Then the boy continued, "When do you think my voice will change?"

Why Parents Get Gray

An altar boy was needed for the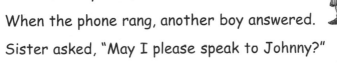
next morning's Mass. Sister Paula
called Johnny to ask him to serve.
When the phone rang, another boy answered.
Sister asked, "May I please speak to Johnny?"

Over the phone she heard the boy yell, "Hey,
Johnny! Some foxy lady wants you on the phone."

Unemployed

Sister Kathleen's first graders were talking about
jobs. They took turns telling what their fathers did.
One boy announced, "My dad doesn't work. He
teaches." Sister was surprised to find out that day
that she wasn't really working.

With Mom's Approval

The students turned in essays on **Catcher in the Rye**. One essay was suspicious. It was not written in the style of the student and was curiously free of spelling errors. Did the girl use Cliff Notes? No. She had used Monarch Notes, copying the opening paragraphs verbatim. When Sister Mary Kathleen met with the plagiarist after school, she began, "About your essay..."

"My mom thought it was really good," the girl broke in.

"Did she know you copied it?" Sister asked.

"My mom liked it," the girl insisted. Then in defense she said, "I changed three words."

"Yes," admitted Sister, "and you added a period that created an incomplete sentence!"

No Room for One More

In the morning the first graders heard about the poor pagan babies in mission lands and how money could be donated to help them. After returning from lunch at home, Marvin proudly came to Sister with pennies in his fist. He declared, "Mommy said I could bring some pennies, but don't let the baby come to our house!"

Principals

A Like Letter

A class from an inner-city school
visited a class in a rural school. A few
days later Sister Virginia, the principal of the host
school, received this note of gratitude: "Dear
Sister, I liked your school in the country. I liked the
dining room and the gym. I liked playing in the snow.
I liked the cows and the pigs. I also liked you."

Hi, God!

St. Anselm's Church is in the center of the school. One Saturday morning Sister Annamae, the CCD principal, was walking through the halls when she saw a tot standing in front of the church doors. Knowing that class had already begun, she asked the child, "Now, who are you?"

"I'm God," came the disconcerting answer.

"And what is God doing out here in the hall?" Sister asked.

"I'm waiting. I have to appear," the child replied.

Only then did Sister remember that the first grade was having a pageant that morning.

Testing the Waters

The kindergarten teacher was not in
her classroom and the children were
taking advantage of it. Hearing
the commotion, Sister Maurene,
the principal, walked to the room
and stood in the doorway.
In her firmest principal
voice she commanded,
"Sit down."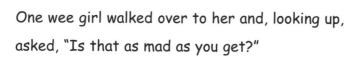

One wee girl walked over to her and, looking up,
asked, "Is that as mad as you get?"

A Secret Life

Little Jamie had frequently come to school with his mother, who worked in the cafeteria. There he often chatted with Sister Jeanne Marie, the principal. Finally the day came when he entered kindergarten. One day he spotted Sister Jeanne Marie in the principal's office.

"What are you doing here?" Jamie asked.

"I'm working," Sister Jeanne Marie answered.

"But why are you in the principal's office?"

"Because I'm the principal," Sister said.

Shocked, Jamie exclaimed, "You mean, all these years I've been talking to the principal?"

Discipline

A Good Excuse

One rambunctious first grader was sent to the principal because he disturbed the other children. He explained to Sister why he was there: "I have restlessness inside me. It's in my blood."

Diagnosis

One lad found it hard to stay seated at his desk and would often wander around the classroom. Finally one of his peers rebuked him, saying, "You must be allergic to your desk."

Getting Attention

Sister Konrad was scolding an incorrigible eighth-grade boy at length. The boy stood staring at her. She thought, "Good. He's finally listening. Maybe this time my words will have an effect." She continued to scold, while the boy stood perfectly still, transfixed, staring at her. Finally, when she took a breath, he said, "Sister, there's a bug crawling in and out of your veil."

The Student Prophet

Joey, a seventh-grade student, was very talkative. One day he tried hard to get Sister Josetta's attention. Finally, she gave in and said, "Yes, Joey, what is it?"

He said, "Sister, when you die, you'll go straight to heaven."

"Why?" Sister asked.

"Because you're patient with me."

Sister answered, "Joey, put that in writing. I may need it."

Breakfast of Losers

Sister Dolores taught high school chemistry. Although barely five feet tall, she rarely had discipline problems. One day, however, she had to reprimand a hefty, six-foot-tall boy. He retorted, "You know, I eat three of you for breakfast!"

Second Thoughts

One morning Jimmy presented his teacher, Sister Marcelita, with a bright, shiny apple. She set it on her desk. During the day, Jimmy misbehaved and Sister had to discipline the little boy. After the children had gone home for the day, Sister noticed that the apple was missing. Apparently Jimmy thought she no longer deserved it.

A Diapered Delinquent

Mrs. C's two girls were well behaved in school. Sister was warned though to get ready for Andrew, who at eleven months was a handful. At Sunday Mass, during the homily, Mrs. C set Andrew on the floor where he played contentedly with her shoe and the kneeler. She turned her attention to the priest. When the homily was over, she glanced down and to her horror Andrew was gone. She scoured the congregation with her eyes, trying to detect any unusual responses. No clue. She looked down once more, and there was Andrew—holding a red, high-heeled shoe.

At communion time Mrs. C found the owner, offered her apologies, and returned the shoe. How did Mrs. C recognize the victim? By watching which woman wobbled up the aisle.

The Downfall

One winter's day, when Sister Julie Rose had playground supervision during recess, the children invented a new game. They were having a great deal of fun falling into the snow on purpose. To prevent injuries and soaking wet clothes, Sister decreed, "The next one who falls into the snow has to go inside." She stepped back, slipped, and fell into the snow. She went inside.

Permanent Bankruptcy

Seven-year-old Justin found it difficult to return library books on time. His fines accumulated until one day he owed a dollar. At the end of the school day his teacher reminded him to bring in money to pay the fine. In all seriousness, a dejected Justin lamented, "Now I won't be able to buy my new car when I'm sixteen."

A Bunch of Baloney

One first grader never got his papers finished. Exasperated, the teacher took him to Sister Jane Therese, the principal, and explained the problem. Sister Jane Therese directed the boy, "Bring your lunch here to the office. You may not go to lunch until you finish your work."

When the boy returned he was put, crying, into a room to do his task. After a short time the door opened, and a wee voice inquired, "How long does it take for baloney sandwiches to spoil?"

"Oh, years and years," Sister replied.

The door closed again, and five minutes later the papers were finished.

A Grim Job

Sister Marc teaches her kindergartners to put all their things away when they are finished with their work. One day Tina left her table a mess. Sister called her back and said, "Tina, throw the scraps into the wastebasket, clean up the floor, and put your crayons and scissors away." Overwhelmed by all this, Tina remarked, "You remind me of Cinderella's stepmother."

Bad Excuse

The snacks were being cleared at the after-school session when Johnny came to Sister Rita and asked for some. "Where were you before?" Sister asked.

"In the bathroom," Johnny replied.

"The whole time?" Sister asked.

"Yes, it takes me a long time."

"Most people don't need such a long time, " Sister countered. "Maybe you'd better see a doctor. How long has this been going on?"

"Oh, about ten years," responded the eight-year-old boy.

Homework, Tests, and Grades

Healthy Self-Esteem

One precocious four-year-old boy asked his teacher to raise his A to an A+. He explained, "Because that's how good I am!"

Spelling Ability

When one first-grade teacher had to give her children an ability test, she thought she'd use psychology to prevent nervousness and fear. She told the children they were going to have a wonderful time with games and puzzles. Suddenly, loud and clear, came a small but emphatic voice: "This is a test, Sister. It says right here, t-e-s-t. That spells **test**."

Fake Punches

At Regina High School, exams were usually multiple-choice questions for which the students indicated their answers by coloring over the letters **a, b, c,** or **d**. To correct the exams easily, teachers made a cover sheet with holes punched out over the right answers.

One day Sister Bernette promised her chemistry students that the one who had the highest score in the review game would receive the answers to the exam as a prize. True to her word, at the end of the game she handed an envelope to the girl who had the most points. In it were all the circles that had been punched out from the cover sheet, each with an **a, b, c,** or **d**.

A Loozing Battle

A new elective course for juniors and seniors was Grammar and Composition. At the end of the first quarter, Sister asked the class to evaluate themselves. One student wrote, "I think I deserve an A cause I didn't no nothing when I started the course." Another student wrote, "I really learned how to wright good."

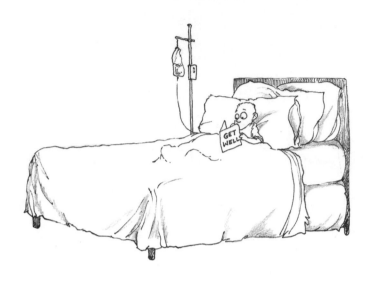

Request of a Bequest

The seventh graders wrote get-well letters to Joe, a bright classmate who was ill. He probably got a little better when he read John's note: "Dear Joe: If you die, can I have your report card?"

Free A's

Sister Nancy tried in vain to get her physics students to read the bulletin boards that she so carefully changed periodically. On the day of the final exam, she announced to her class, "I'm sure you'll have no problem with this exam. All week long it's been posted on the bulletin board with the answers." The class screamed.

Christmas Cut-ups

The More the Merrier

The fourth graders were learning about the season of Advent. Sister Barbara asked, "Why do you think God waited four thousand years before he sent a Savior?" The creative answer came, "He wanted to stock up on people."

Christmas Charades

Sister Domicele's fourth-grade class was exceptionally spontaneous. When the students were practicing "O Holy Night," their song for the Christmas program, they complained that one line was really hard. "Which one?" Sister asked. With that, the students stood up, and then fell on their knees.

John Was There

Before Christmas the first graders were drawing pictures of the nativity. When Sister Lisette looked at one boy's artwork, she recognized Mary and Joseph and the crib with Baby Jesus in it. She also identified a shepherd. However, one figure puzzled her. Standing next to the stable was a very fat boy. "Who is this?" she asked.

"Oh, that's round John Virgin," the artist explained.

A Giant Elf

During recess and between classes, one Sister crocheted small items as Christmas gifts for her children. One of her students asked what she was doing. "You never ask Santa's elves what they are doing," Sister replied.

Glancing at his 5-foot-9-inch teacher, the little boy was puzzled. He remarked, "You're too big to be an elf."

Saints

Saint Charade

One eighth grader refused to take notes as his class viewed filmstrips on the lives of the saints. He insisted that he could remember the material. Later, a quiz proved him wrong when he made these identifications: St. Martian Despress (for Martin de Porres)—He cured people and then they died; St. Catherine of Siena—She cut off her hair, and then she became a noun. (The teacher, Sister Andrew, thought Catherine was more like a verb!)

Living Saint

Sister Mary Beth took her first graders to the church for a tour. The children were fascinated by the large stained-glass window depicting Pentecost. It showed the Holy Spirit coming down upon Mary and the apostles. One child whispered, "Sister, where are you in the picture?"

Extra Credit

Two weeks before the Feast of All Saints, the children at school were given a set of fifty riddles about saints to solve with their families. One father, who was a college history professor, was determined that his family get 100% and be the first to turn in the completed page. The next morning he told his college students, "If I'm a little incoherent today, please excuse me. I was up until 3:00 a.m. doing my children's homework. Now tell me, who is the patron saint of hatmakers?"

Saint Defaming

Sister Jude Andrew had her children learn something about their patron saints. On the day itself the parish priest paid a visit. Father asked little Frank, "Who is your patron?"

"St. Francis," came the reply.

"Good," said Father. "Do you know anything about your patron saint?"

"Oh, yes, Father," Frank said. "He was a sissy." The boy apparently had not persevered long in his research of St. Francis of Assisi.

Food for Thought

In preparation for the Feast of All Saints the first and second graders were discussing heaven. Lacey said, "There must be an awfully long table in heaven for all those people. And it's going to take forever to pass the mashed potatoes."

Alex tried to dispel her concerns. He said, "I heard that our plates will be full when they are put in front of us."

Not one to stop worrying, Lacey replied, "But what will we do for seconds?"

Sacraments and Sacramentals

Branded

A fourth grade student, unfamiliar with the Catholic ritual of Ash Wednesday, nervously asked his teacher, "Are the ashes hot?"

A Lesson That Got Home

Mr. and Mrs. Brown took turns driving the Sisters to teach CCD on Saturdays. One morning Mrs. Brown told this story:

She and Mr. Brown were having a discussion. At one point the conversation was becoming a little heated. Suddenly, little Suzie, who had recently made her first confession, interrupted.

"Daddy," she said, "now you apologize to Mommy!"

Quite taken aback, Mr. Brown asked, "Why?"

Suzie explained, "Because you've started an argument with Mommy." Mr. Brown then apologized. But little Suzie wasn't going to let her father off so easily. In a serious tone she continued, "Now, Daddy, you know it's not enough to just say you're sorry. You have to try really hard never to do it again."

"That does it," said Mr. Brown. "Next week the Sisters walk to school!"

Saturated with Grace

A second-grader had bought a medal and a chain at a religious goods sale. Concerned that it be a real sacramental, he asked, "Sister, is my medal blessed, or must I take it home and soak it in holy water?"

Joy Genes

After the CCD children made their first holy communion, one little boy was going to join his mother and father. He was beaming with happiness. Someone asked him, "What makes you so happy?" He gave it some thought, then came up with the answer, "I guess it just runs in our family."

Smart Girl

Some children were acting out a wedding ceremony. The priest asked the bride, "Do you take him for better or worse?"

"For better," the little girl said quickly.

The priest continued, "For richer or poorer?"

"For richer," stated the miniature bride.

Prayer

Divine Affirmation

During the first graders' religion class, Sister invited, "Now let's close our eyes and listen to what God is saying to us." It was quiet. After a short time, Sister asked, "Can anyone tell us what God said to you?" One hand went up, and a small boy said, "Kevin, you're my best invention."

Education Gap

In preparing her second graders for the sacrament of reconciliation, Sister Karlene taught them about penance. She explained, "Father might say to you, 'For your penance, say five Our Fathers.'"

After class one little boy remained at his desk crying. When Sister asked the reason for his tears, he sobbed, "I only know one Our Father, not the other four."

Semi-Contrition

A second grader, reciting the Act of Contrition, prayed, "O my God, I am partly sorry..."

A Swear Prayer

A first grader was caught praying, "Hell, Mary"—quite an understandable mistake if you've never heard the word **Hail** before.

A Happy Ending

When November 2 came along, the second grade learned about the poor souls in purgatory. At least one child remembered the lesson. A few days later, during the morning prayers of petition, Andrea prayed, "For the repose of the soul of my uncle. He was killed in a car accident but is doing much better now."

Rote Prayers

Despite the school rule that no children may enter the building during recess, two young girls went to the principal's office one day, very excited. "Sister Regina," they said. "We saw the Blessed Virgin above the garages."

"Oh," said Sister. "Did you tell the teacher out there?"

"Yes," the girls nodded their heads. "She saw Mary, too."

Deciding that this needed to be investigated, Sister Regina went outside and walked over to the teacher.

"Yes," the teacher confirmed, "some clouds did look like they were in the shape of the Blessed Virgin."

Turning to the two girls, Sister Regina asked, "What did you do when you saw Mary?"

"Well," one girl replied, "we said our first communion prayers, then we prayed a Hail Mary, and then we said the Pledge of Allegiance to the Flag."

Hodgepodge

A New Emily Post

Sister Barbara was teaching her seventh graders the etiquette rules for making introductions, such as the younger is presented to the older and the less important is presented to the more important. Donna shared her own rule with her classmates: "I go by the wrinkles."

The Cinderella Desk

One day a new student was assigned to Sister Immaculee's third-grade class. There were no more desks except for one in storage that left much to be desired. Its legs were bent, the wood was scarred, and the metal was rusted. No student would want such a desk, and the student, if assigned to sit at it, would probably complain to his or her parents.

Then Sister had a brilliant idea. She introduced the desk to the class as the honor desk. The student who made the biggest improvement each week could sit there. For the rest of the year the children vied to be the honored person to occupy that desk.

All <u>What</u>?

The parish priest liked to wear pullover sweaters. While visiting Sister Sharon's second-grade class, his eye was attracted to one fellow's sweater.

"Do you think I could borrow your sweater sometime?" Father teased the boy.

"Sure," the lad generously responded, "one size fits all."

A Logical Conclusion

A new modular unit was stationed close to the school for special classes. A child seeing it for the first time remarked to a friend, "And here's the Sisters' new camper."

Delayed Reaction

Sister Constant laid down a firm rule for her young students: If they forgot their gym clothes, they could not have gym. No gym clothes, no gym.

A few days later, when the children were supposed to change into their gym clothes, one boy did not move. He sat there crying, his gym clothes nowhere in sight. When Sister went to the distraught boy, he looked up and said defensively, "I'm not crying because I forgot my gym clothes."

"Oh? Then why are you crying?" Sister asked.

"Because my grandfather died," the tyke replied.

A bit suspicious, Sister questioned, "And when did your grandfather die?"

"Five years ago," the boy said.

The Importance
of Previews

As moderator of the Athletics Association, Sister
Mary Marthe had planned to show three hundred
girls **Fundamentals of Good Bowling** in an activity
period. On the scheduled day, the movie still hadn't
arrived, and Sister was nervous. Sister Dina, the
school secretary, told her, "If it comes, I'll let you
know."

During the morning, Sister Dina called for Sister
and said, "Don't worry. The film's here. I'll have it on
the projector all set to go for you."

During the activity period, as students pulled down
the black shades in the auditorium, Sister Marthe
explained that the movie would teach them very

basic things that would make the difference between a good bowler and a bad one.

She turned on the projector, and a lady in a pink negligee appeared on the screen. The woman asked, "Do you know if you need a two-way stretch girdle, a panty-girdle, or just a garter belt? Do you need a front-laced corset or a back-laced one? Do you wear cup size A, B, or C?" Immediately Sister Marthe flicked off the projector, while the auditorium rang with screams of laughter. The film, which obviously had been placed in the wrong canister, was entitled **How to Select a Foundation**.

A Recycled Library

The school library project involved a number of fundraisers to get money for books. One Sunday an announcement in the church bulletin read, "School News: We are building our library from rags and empty pop bottles. Please bring these discarded items to the church lounge."

Drill Resistant

During fire prevention week the school had a number of fire drills—too many for sixth-grader Mickey. He was weary of going outside every time the fire bell rang. When the bell sounded yet again, Mickey requested, "Sister, just make like I'm a nonburnable for this next one, okay?"